T·H·E B·E·S·T O·F
SUMMER
FRUITS

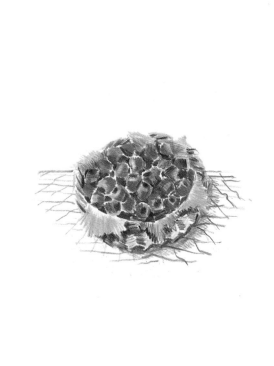

T·H·E B·E·S·T O·F
SUMMER
FRUITS

GARAMOND

First published by Garamond Ltd, Publishers
Strode House, 44–50 Osnaburgh Street, London NW1 3ND

Copyright © Garamond Ltd, Publishers 1990

ISBN 1-85583-045-0

Illustrations by Madeleine David

Typeset by Bookworm Ltd.
Printed and bound in the UK by MacLehose and Partners Ltd.

CONTENTS

Introduction · 8
Apricot chicken soup · 12
Berry soup · 14
Pork chops in apricot sauce · 16
Lamb polo · 18
Peach salad · 20
Fresh raspberry cream · 21
Raspberry mousse · 22
Apricot almond sweets · 24
Nutty peach tart · 25
Peach parfait · 26
Peaches in brandy · 27
Italian summer dessert · 28
Grilled nectarines · 29
Peach meringue pie · 30
Quick and easy sauce · 33
Apricot cream · 34
Raspberry sauce · 36
Redcurrant and mint sauce · 36
Kentish country jam · 37
Vin d'apricot · 38
Raspberry cordial · 40
Apricot moisturizing mask · 41
Measurements · 42

INTRODUCTION

Apricots, peaches and raspberries are among the best of summer fruits, with their taste and look of summer days; and all three can be used in a variety of recipes created to highlight and enhance their natural flavours.

Apricots are thought to have come originally from China but early on they were introduced into the Near East, hence their botanical name, *Prunus armenica*. Since those days they have spread all over the world and appear in all kinds of dishes, from soups to sweets.

To freeze apricots, halve or slice them and freeze in a syrup made from 450 grams (1 lb) sugar to 1.1 litres (2 pints) water; add 50 grams (2 ounces) ascorbic acid for each 550 ml (pint) syrup. Plunge the whole apricots into boiling water first for about thirty seconds, and peel.

They are one of the best natural sources of Vitamin A, especially when dried.

Fresh peaches are cheap and plentiful throughout the summer months, and may be yellow or white fleshed. They can be used in soups and as a garnish (for baked ham and roast duckling) as well as sweets and in ice creams. Soft, ripe peaches are best eaten just as they are – and must anyway be used as quickly as possible: decay spreads very fast.

To peel peaches, pour boiling water over a few fruits at a time, and leave for 1 or 2 minutes to loosen their skin. Then, hold each peach in a soft kitchen cloth and strip off its skin. If this is done with care, faint markings of colour will remain on the surface of the peeled fruit. Halve the peaches lengthwise and remove stains.

Peel and stone the fruit before freezing, brush halves or slices with lemon juice and use a syrup made from 450 grams (1 lb) to every 550 grams (pint) water.

Peach juice is soothing and diuretic – and an excellent moisturizer.

Raspberries are ripe when they are brightly and evenly coloured, and slip easily off their hulls. Ideally, they should be used as soon as they have been picked as they rapidly turn mouldy.

Wash them only when absolutely necessary, and then only give them the slightest of sprays with water. If they are not to be used immediately, they may be stored in the bottom of the refrigerator before cleaning, but bring them out well in advance of serving.

Fine raspberries need no accompaniment apart from a sprinkling of sugar. You can also serve them with lightly whipped cream flavoured with orange liqueur or Kirsch, or with dollops of vanilla ice cream.

Freeze them whole on a baking sheet in a single layer then pack them into cartons or bags; if space is limited, purée them first. This gives you the opportunity to use up any squashed or crumbled fruit. Sweeten the purée lightly before it goes into the freezer but be prepared to adjust the flavour with more sugar before using it.

Redcurrants, while not as widely available as other summer fruits, have a unique flavour that makes them ideal for tangy sauces and jellies to serve with roasts of lamb, poultry and game birds, as glazes for brushing over pastries, cakes and open fruit tarts, or added (in small amounts) to fresh vegetables and fruit salads.

Sugar freeze redcurrants whole. If you cook the fruit it is worthwhile putting it through a fine sieve to eliminate their many pips. Dry or sugar freeze the whole fruits.

APRICOT CHICKEN SOUP

350–450 grams (¾–1 lb) chicken joints
Salt
1 chicken stock cube (optional)
100–125 grams (4 oz) short-grain rice, rinsed and drained
175 grams (6 oz) potato, peeled and diced
100–125 grams (4 oz) plump dried apricots, rinsed and cut
into strips
Freshly ground black pepper
Ground cinnamon
150 millilitres (¼ pint) single cream
4 tablespoons finely chopped fresh dill or parsley

Rinse chicken joints and put them in a large pan. Sprinkle
with salt and cover with 1.7 litres (3 pints) cold water. Add
a crumbled chicken cube if liked at this stage. Slowly bring
to boiling point and simmer for 20 minutes. Skim surface
clear of any scum and fat.
Stir in rice, diced potato, apricots, and a generous pinch
each of freshly ground black pepper and cinnamon.
Simmer until the ingredients are quite soft and chicken
meat is falling off the bones.

With a slotted spoon, lift out chicken joints. Bone them, sliver meat and return to the soup. Stir in cream. Correct seasoning if necessary. Bring to just below boiling point and serve, each portion sprinkled with chopped dill or parsley.

Serves 6–8

BERRY SOUP

450 grams (1 lb) mixed berries: raspberries, strawberries,
blackberries etc, as available
400 millilitres (¾ pint) single cream
700 millilitres (1¼ pints) milk
300 millilitres (½ pint) thick sour cream
About 50 grams (2 oz) caster sugar
Lemon juice
Ice cubes and sugared croûtons, to serve

Rub the fruits through a fine sieve or vegetable mouli, or
purée them in an electric blender and then sieve out the
seeds.

Blend the cream, milk and sour cream together with the
puréed fruit. Sweeten to taste, and if necessary intensify
the flavour with a little lemon juice.

Chill the soup until ready to serve. Serve in a large tureen
with a few ice cubes floating in it to keep it chilled
throughout the course, and accompanied by a bowl of
sugared croûtons to sprinkle over each portion.

Serves 8

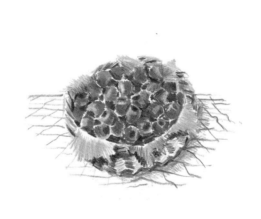

PORK CHOPS IN APRICOT SAUCE

225 grams (8 oz) dried apricots
300 millilitres (½ pint) dry white wine or cider
6 thick pork chops
Seasoned flour
1 onion, finely chopped
3 tablespoons oil
2 tablespoons soft brown sugar
2 tablespoons coarsely chopped blanched almonds or walnuts

Rinse the apricots thoroughly under the cold tap. Put them in a bowl, cover with wine or cider and leave to soak overnight.

The following day, trim pork chops of any excess fat and dust them all over with well-seasoned flour. Remove about a quarter of the apricots from the wine and blend the remainder together with the wine to a smooth purée in an electric blender or food processor. Chop the whole apricots coarsely and stir them into the purée.

In a large frying pan, simmer the onion in half the oil until soft and golden. Remove the onion with a slotted spoon and put aside until needed. Heat the remaining oil in the frying pan and fry the chops, 2 or 3 at a time, until golden brown on both sides. Transfer them to an ovenproof casserole as they are done, making two layers in all and sprinkling each layer with some of the sautéed onion.

Deglaze the pan with 6–8 tablespoons water, stirring and

scraping the surface clean with a wooden spoon. Bring to the boil and pour over the chops. Cover with the apricot purée.

Put on the lid and bake in a moderate oven (180°C, 350°F, Mark 4) until chops are quite tender, about 1 hour. For the last 15 minutes of baking time, remove the lid, sprinkle the surface with a mixture of sugar and nuts, and continue baking until sugar has melted and surface is bubbling. Serve from the casserole.

Serves 6

LAMB POLO

---

2 Spanish onions, finely chopped
50 grams (2 oz) butter
900 grams (2 lbs) lean boned lamb, cubed
Salt and freshly ground black pepper
½–1 teaspoon ground cinnamon
225 grams (8 oz) plump dried apricots, quartered
6–8 tablespoons seedless raisins
About 400 millilitres (¾ pint) light chicken (cube) stock
Juice of ½ lemon
1–2 tablespoons apricot preserve, to taste

In a heavy pan or flameproof casserole, sauté onions gently in butter until transparent and lightly coloured. Transfer to a plate with a slotted spoon. In the remaining butter, brown the lamb cubes all over, a portion at a time. Return the onions and all the lamb to the pan. Season lightly with salt, pepper and cinnamon, and stir in the apricots and raisins. Sauté gently for a few minutes longer. Pour in hot chicken stock (or water) to cover. Bring slowly to simmering point, cover the pan and cook gently for about 2 hours until the lamb is tender and the apricots soft and pulpy, adding more stock if it evaporates too quickly.

Half an hour before the lamb is ready, flavour to taste with lemon juice and apricot preserve.
Just before serving, correct seasoning, and add a little more cinnamon if liked.

Serves 6

PEACH SALAD

4 large, ripe peaches
Juice of 1 large lemon
50 grams (2 oz) caster sugar
1–2 tablespoons coarsely chopped, skinned and toasted hazelnuts,
or toasted flaked almonds

Peel peaches. Cut them in half lengthwise and remove stones. Crack stones open, remove kernels and chop them finely. In a small bowl, stir lemon juice and sugar together until sugar has melted. Stir in chopped peach kernels. Slice peaches into a glass serving bowl. Pour sweetened lemon juice over slices and turn them gently until coated on all sides. Sprinkle with nuts and chill before serving.

Serves 4

FRESH RASPBERRY CREAM

---

300 millilitres (½ pint) lightly sweetened raspberry purée
3–4 tablespoons Framboise or Kirsch
2 large egg whites
Pinch of salt
About 3–4 tablespoons caster sugar
400 millilitres (¾ pint) double cream

Flavour the raspberry purée with Framboise or Kirsch and put aside until needed.

In a large, clean, dry bowl, beat the egg whites with a pinch of salt until they form soft, floppy peaks when beaters are lifted. Gradually adding 3 tablespoons sugar, continue to beat to a stiff, glossy meringue. In a separate bowl, beat cream until it is thick but not buttery.

Fold egg whites into whipped cream, followed by raspberry purée. Taste and add a little more sugar if needed to sweeten.

Pour mixture into a freezer tray or plastic bowl. Cover with a lid or a sheet of foil. Freeze until firm.

Transfer the container to the main compartment of the refrigerator about 1 hour before serving to soften slightly.

Serves 6

RASPBERRY MOUSSE

450 grams (1 lb) fresh raspberries or 575 grams (1¼ lbs) frozen
raspberries
15 grams (½ oz) powdered gelatine
300 millilitres (½ pint) double cream
4 tablespoons caster sugar
4 eggs, separated
100–125 grams (4 oz) almond macaroons
Whipped cream and whole raspberries, to decorate

If using frozen raspberries, thaw them in a sieve set over a
bowl to allow any juices to drip away. Then, in a food
processor or blender, purée fruit. Press purée through a
fine nylon sieve and discard pips. Put aside. Sprinkle
gelatine over 2 or 3 tablespoons water (or the juice that
drained from the thawing raspberries) in a cup and allow
to soften, then solidify. Stand cup in a small pan of very
hot water and stir until gelatine has dissolved and liquid is
quite clear. Cool to lukewarm.

In the top of a double saucepan, or a heatproof bowl that
will fit snugly over a pan of simmering water, beat cream,
sugar and egg yolks together until fluffy and well blended.
Fit pan over simmering water and continue to beat until
custard has thickened. Remove pan from lower container
and continue beating lightly until custard has cooled to
lukewarm. Then stir in dissolved gelatine and raspberry
purée until thoroughly blended. Allow to cool until syrupy
but not set, stirring occasionally to prevent a skin forming
on top.

Beat egg whites until they form soft peaks and fold them into the cold raspberry custard. Crush macaroons to crumbs (in a plastic bag with a rolling pin is easiest) and fold them in as well.

Spoon mousse into a glass serving bowl and chill until quite set. Serve decorated with swirls of whipped cream and a few whole raspberries.

Serves 6

APRICOT ALMOND SWEETS

225 grams (8 oz) plump dried apricots
Caster sugar or sifted icing sugar
1 tablespoon ground almonds (optional)
1–2 drops almond essence (optional)
Slivered blanched almonds or peeled pistachio nuts, to decorate

Wash the apricots and dry them thoroughly. Put them through the fine blade of a meat mincer, or twice if necessary through the coarser blade, to reduce them to a rather coarse paste. Sweeten to taste with sugar and mix in the ground almonds and almond essence if used. Work the paste with your fingertips until ingredients are smoothly blended.

Sprinkle a board lined with greaseproof paper with an even layer of sugar. Roll the apricot paste into marble-sized balls, coat them with sugar and leave to dry and harden overnight.

The following day, decorate each sweet with a few almond slivers or a peeled pistachio nut. Place in little paper cases and serve with after-dinner coffee.

Note: If the apricot paste is too dry to roll into smooth balls, it can be moistened with a few drops of lemon juice or cold water.

NUTTY PEACH TART

One 20 or 22.5 centimetre (8 or 9 in.) shortcrust pastry case,
pre-baked
450 grams (1 lb) fresh, ripe peaches
3 eggs
100–125 grams (4 oz) ground almonds
100 -125 grams (4 oz) icing sugar, sifted
Flaked almonds, to decorate (optional)

Bake the case very lightly, just long enough to set the pastry without colouring it. Leave the pastry case in its tin or flan ring on a baking sheet.

Peel peaches. Cut them in half lengthwise, remove stones and either leave them in halves or cut each half into 6 or 8 slices, depending on size. Arrange peaches neatly in case.

Beat eggs until fluffy. Gently fold in ground almonds and icing sugar until thoroughly mixed. Pour evenly over peaches and sprinkle with a few flaked almonds if available. Bake tart in a moderate oven (190°C, 375°F, Mark 5) until filling is set and a rich golden colour, about 30 minutes. Serve lukewarm or cold.

Serves 6

PEACH PARFAIT

4 large ripe peaches
100–125 grams (4 oz) sugar
Pinch of salt
3 egg yolks, beaten well
150 millilitres (¼ pint) whipping cream

Peel peaches. Remove the stones and chop the fruit into small pieces, then push these through a fine sieve (or use a blender) to make a purée.

Place 150 millilitres (¼ pint) water, sugar and salt in the top of a double boiler or in a basin over a pan of boiling water. Cook, stirring constantly until the sugar dissolves. Then add the beaten egg yolks. Continue beating the mixture as it cooks over the hot water, until it thickens (do not allow to boil). Then beat in the peach purée and cook for a further 2 minutes, stirring constantly. Remove the pan from the heat and stand the basin containing the mixture in a bowl of cold water. Whisk for a few minutes as it cools. In another bowl, whip the cream until it is light and airy, but not stiff, then fold this into the peach mixture. Pour into a freezing tray and freeze. This should take about 3 hours, and the parfait does not need stirring during this time.

Serves 4–6

PEACHES IN BRANDY

900 grams (2 lbs) ripe, unblemished peaches
225 grams (8 oz) sugar
about 150 millilitres (¼ pint) brandy

Peel the peaches, halve them vertically and remove stones.
Cut each peach half into 6 or 8 thin slices.
In a wide, shallow pan, dissolve sugar in 550 millilitres
(1 pint) water to make a light syrup. Drop the peach slices
into the simmering syrup and poach gently until just
cooked and still very firm. With a slotted spoon, transfer
slices to hot, clean jars.
Boil syrup briskly until thickened and reduced to about
one-third of the original amount. Strain it through a fine
sieve. Measure out about 150 millilitres (¼ pint) and stir in
an equal amount of brandy.
Drain off any syrup that has accumulated in the jars of
peaches. Then slowly pour in brandied syrup, wait a few
minutes for it to 'settle', and top up with more, covering
the peaches completely.
Cover jars as usual and store in a cool, dry cupboard.
Leave for several weeks before tasting to allow flavours
to develop.

ITALIAN SUMMER DESSERT

4 large firm ripe peaches
50 grams (2 oz) amaretti or macaroons
25 grams (1 oz) almonds, blanched and peeled
4 tablespoons caster sugar
1 tablespoon unsweetened cocoa powder
4–6 tablespoons white wine
Butter, for baking dish
Chilled pouring cream, to serve (optional)

Cut peaches in half lengthwise and remove stones. Break stones open, remove kernels and chop them finely. Place in a bowl. Hollow out peach cavities slightly to make room for filling. Chop up scooped-out pulp and add to bowl.

Crumble amaretti or macaroons and stir them into bowl. Split 4 of the almonds in half and reserve for decoration. Chop remainder finely and add to bowl. Stir in 3 tablespoons sugar and the cocoa powder. Moisten with 2 or 3 tablespoons wine and work to a paste.

Stuff each peach cavity with some of the paste, rounding it up and smoothing it over with a knife blade. Arrange peach halves side by side in a lightly buttered baking dish. Sprinkle them with remaining sugar and top each half-peach with an almond flake. Moisten with remaining wine. Bake peaches in a moderate oven (190°C, 375°F, Mark 5) for 25–30 minutes, until peaches have softened and mounds of stuffing are crisp and crusty on top.

Serve 2 peach halves per person while they are still very warm, accompanied by chilled, unsweetened pouring cream if liked.

Serves 4

GRILLED NECTARINES

A good way to use nectarines that are too hard to eat raw. Halve and stone nectarines. Lay the halves on a baking sheet, cut side up; sprinkle with brown sugar, dot with flecks of butter, and grill for 5–7 minutes until the butter and sugar have caramelized into a bubbling brown topping.
Serve hot with chilled cream.

PEACH MERINGUE PIE

Meringue
4 egg whites
¼ teaspoon cream of tartar
225 grams (8 oz) caster sugar

Peaches and cream filling
4 egg yolks
100–125 grams (4 oz) caster sugar
Pinch of salt
Finely grated rind and juice of 1 large lemon
300 millilitres (½ pint) double cream or 150 millilitres (¼ pint) each
double and single cream, mixed
4–5 ripe peaches

Prepare the meringue shell well in advance. The preceding day will probably be the most convenient. First, line a baking sheet with silicone paper or a sheet of greaseproof paper lightly brushed with a wad of kitchen paper dipped in tasteless oil. On the lining paper, mark a circle 22.5 centimetres (9 in.) in diameter as a guide for the shell. In a large bowl that is spotlessly clean and dry, whisk egg whites until just frothy. Sprinkle with cream of tartar and whisk to soft peak stage. Then gradually whisk in sugar and continue to whisk to a stiff, glossy meringue.

Shape meringue into a 22.5 centimetre (9 in.) nest, either using a piping bag fitted with a large, plain nozzle, or in a far simpler (and less messy) way as follows. With a tablespoon, scoop up balls of meringue and place them

around sides of circle. Then fill the centre of the circle with more meringue and with the back of your spoon, smooth it out to form a nest. Finally, if you like, rough up the surface (neatly and regularly) with a skewer or the prongs of a large kitchen fork.

Let the meringue shell dry out in a cool oven (140°C, 275°F, Mark 1) for at least 1 hour, or until it is hard and brittle, and very lightly tinged with gold. Then turn off the oven, leaving the meringue in it for several hours or overnight to cool completely.

Prepare cream filling. In the top of a double saucepan, beat egg yolks just enough to mix them and make them foamy. Lightly beat in sugar, salt and the grated lemon rind and juice. Fit top of pan over simmering water and stir constantly until mixture is very thick and creamy. Take care not to let it boil or egg yolks will curdle. Cool, giving it an occasional stir to prevent a skin forming on top.

Whisk cream until it stands in light, floppy peaks. Put aside about 4 large tablespoonfuls in a small bowl or cup for decoration. Gently but thoroughly fold remainder into cream filling. Chill lightly.

Peel and stone peaches, and slice them lengthwise. Pick out about 8 of the best slices for decoration.

Assemble the meringue pie as follows. Peel off lining paper and lay meringue case on a large, flat serving dish. Spread evenly with a thin layer of cream filling. Cover closely with slices of peach. Then spread remaining filling over the top. Decorate with reserved peach slices and dollops of whipped cream. Chill lightly until ready to serve but serve as soon as possible.

Serves 8

QUICK AND EASY SAUCE

One 400 gram (14 oz) can apricots in syrup
About 1 tablespoon sugar
1 teaspoon arrowroot or potato flour
About 1 tablespoon lemon juice
1–2 teaspoons Kirsch, orange liqueur or brandy (optional)
Icing sugar (optional)

Drain apricots, reserving syrup. Put them in an electric blender or food processor. Sprinkle with sugar and blend to a smooth purée. Pour into a small pan.

Blend arrowroot or potato flour smoothly with 3 or 4 tablespoons reserved syrup and stir into apricot purée, together with the lemon juice. Bring to boiling point and simmer, stirring, for 3 or 4 minutes until sauce has thickened and no longer tastes of raw starch.

If sauce is to be served hot, thin it down with a little more of the reserved syrup if too thick, then taste and add more sugar or lemon juice if liked. If it is to be a cold sauce, let it cool after it has been thickened, then stir in liqueur or brandy if used, and finally adjust sweetness with a little icing sugar (which dissolves most easily) if necessary.

APRICOT CREAM

225 grams (8 oz) dried apricots, soaked overnight
75 grams (3 oz) granulated sugar
6–8 tablespoons Madeira
Lemon juice (optional)
2 egg whites
75 grams (3 oz) caster sugar
150 millilitres (¼ pint) whipping cream

Pour the apricots and their soaking water into a pan. Stir
in granulated sugar and 2 or 3 tablespoons more water if
necessary so that fruit are barely covered. Bring to boiling
point and simmer until apricots are very soft. Drain them
thoroughly. Pour cooking juices back into the pan and boil
until reduced to a few tablespoons of thick syrup. Stir into
apricots and leave until cold.
Add Madeira to apricots and whirl to a smooth, thick
purée in an electric blender or food processor. Taste, and
blend in a little more sugar, Madeira or a squeeze of lemon
juice if liked. The purée should be well flavoured but must
remain thick.

Whisk the egg whites until they form soft, floppy peaks when beaters are lifted. Gradually whisk in caster sugar and continue to whisk to a stiff, glossy meringue. Whisk cream lightly.

Fold meringue into apricot purée, followed by whipped cream. Spoon into a glass serving bowl or into individual dishes and chill until ready to serve.

Serves 6

RASPBERRY SAUCE

450 grams (1 lb) fresh or thawed frozen raspberries
Lemon juice
Icing sugar

Rub raspberries through a fine nylon sieve and discard seeds. Beat in lemon juice and icing sugar to taste (2 or 3 tablespoons of each should be enough) and chill lightly until ready to serve.

REDCURRANT AND MINT SAUCE

2 tablespoons redcurrant jelly
1 tablespoon finely chopped fresh mint
Juice and finely grated rind of ½ orange

Put the redcurrant jelly in a bowl and break it into small pieces with a wooden spoon. Add the chopped mint, orange juice and rind. Mix together thoroughly and chill before serving.

KENTISH COUNTRY JAM

1.6 kilograms (3½ lbs) slightly under-ripe fresh apricots
Juice of 1 large lemon
1 teaspoon finely grated lemon rind
1.4 kilograms (3 lbs) sugar

Wash the apricots, stone them and put them through the coarse blade of a meat mincer. In a preserving pan, combine the apricots with the lemon juice and rind, and stir in the sugar. Leave for an hour or two to allow sugar to draw out the apricot juices. (If there doesn't seem to be enough, you could add up to 150 millilitres (¼ pint) water.)

Place the pan over low heat and stir frequently until sugar has dissolved. Then raise heat, bring to boiling point and boil rapidly, stirring frequently, until jam has thickened and setting point is reached. Skim off any scum that forms on the surface.

Cool slightly. Pot and cover.

Fills about 5 jars

VIN D'APRICOT

1.8 kilograms (4 lbs) fresh apricots, or 450 grams (1 lb) dried
apricots
225 grams (8 oz) chopped sultanas
1 Campden tablet
1 teaspoon Pectozyme
1 teacup cold strong tea
1 nutrient tablet
Burgundy yeast
1.1 kilograms (2½ lbs) granulated sugar

Wash the fruit. If you are using fresh apricots, discard the stones, but do not remove the skin. Chop the fruit into small pieces and place it in the prepared mashing vessel. Add the sultanas, Campden tablet, Pectozyme and 4.5 litres (1 gallon) water. Cover the vessel and then leave it for 24 hours.

Quickly uncover the mashing vessel and add the strong tea, the nutrient tablet and the activated yeast (see manufacturer's instructions for quantity and method of use). Replace the lid and leave for 7 days in a warm place (18–24°C or 65–75°F). During this period, stir once a day to ensure that all the fruit is kept moist. Do this quickly and always make sure the vessel is firmly covered at all other times.

Using a fine sieve, strain off the liquid into a clean container. Put the remaining fruit pulp into a linen bag. Seal the bag tightly and squeeze out as much juice as possible into the same container. Stir in the sugar and quickly siphon into a prepared fermentation vessel, filling to within 2.5 cm (1 in.) of the cork. Leave to ferment under an air-lock in a warm place (18–24°C or 65–75°F). This will take approximately 3 weeks.

Rack, store for at least 6 months, and bottle in the usual way. It is advisable to keep this wine for at least a year, before drinking.

Makes 4.5 litres
(1 gallon)

RASPBERRY CORDIAL

900 grams (2 lbs) ripe, fresh raspberries
1.7 litres (3 pints) vodka
900 grams (2 lbs) granulated sugar

Pick over and wash the fruit, then crush the berries slightly. Pack into a large, wide-necked, screw-top jar (a Kilner jar is ideal) and pour over the vodka. Seal the jar and leave to stand in a cool place for 1 month, shaking occasionally.

At the end of this time, make a syrup by dissolving the sugar in 550 millilitres (1 pint) water and boiling for 15 minutes. Open the jar containing the fruit and alcohol and strain off the liquid through a fine sieve into a clean bowl, pressing the fruit to extract as much juice as possible. Stir the sugar syrup into the fruit liqueur. Bottle and leave for 6 months before drinking.

Makes about 2 litres
(3½ pints)

APRICOT
MOISTURIZING MASK

The Vitamin A content of apricots is especially beneficial
to dry skins. Either fresh or dried fruit is suitable.

If using fresh apricots, simply remove the stones and mash
the fruit; if using dried, soak for an hour or so in water
before chopping finely and mashing. Mix the fruit pulp
with enough oil (olive, safflower, peanut, avocado or
almond) to make a spreadable paste.

Clean your face thoroughly, and pat the paste on, avoiding
the area under the eyes. Leave on for about 20 minutes,
then wash off gently with warm water.

MEASUREMENTS

Quantities have been given in both metric and imperial measures in this book. However, many foodstuffs are now available only in metric quantities; the list below gives metric measures for weight and liquid capacity, and their imperial equivalents used in this book.

WEIGHT

25 grams	1 oz
50 grams	2 oz
75 grams	3 oz
100–125 grams	4 oz
150 grams	5 oz
175 grams	6 oz
200 grams	7 oz
225 grams	8 oz
250 grams	9 oz
275 grams	10 oz
300 grams	11 oz
350 grams	12 oz
375 grams	13 oz

400 grams	14 oz
425 grams	15 oz
450 grams	1 lb
500 grams (½ kilogram)	1 lb 1½ oz
1 kilogram	2 lb 3 oz
1.5 kilograms	3 lb 5 oz
2 kilograms	4 lb 6 oz
2.5 kilograms	5 lb 8 oz
3 kilograms	6 lb 10 oz
3.5 kilograms	7 lb 11 oz
4 kilograms	8 lb 13 oz
4.5 kilograms	9 lb 14 oz
5 kilograms	11 lb

LIQUID CAPACITY

150 millilitres	¼ pint
300 millilitres	½ pint
425 millilitres	¾ pint
550–600 millilitres	1 pint
900 millilitres	1½ pints
1000 millilitres (1 litre)	1¾ pints
1.2 litres	2 pints
1.3 litres	2¼ pints
1.4 litres	2½ pints
1.5 litres	2¾ pints
1.9 litres	3¼ pints
2 litres	3½ pints
2.5 litres	4½ pints

OVEN TEMPERATURES

Very low	130°C, 250°F, Mark ½
Low	140°C, 275°F, Mark 1
Very slow	150°C, 300°F, Mark 2
Slow	170°C, 325°F, Mark 3
Moderate	180°C, 350°F, Mark 4
	190°C, 375°F, Mark 5
Moderately hot	200°C, 400°F, Mark 6
Fairly hot	220°C, 425°F, Mark 7
Hot	230°C, 450°F, Mark 8

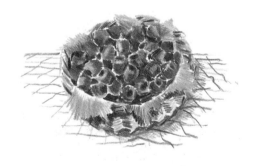